THINGS I'LL NEVER SAY

A collection of streams of consciousness
through a healing journey shared with you
in the hopes that you feel less alone.

MICAELA ELISE

Things I'll Never Say

Copyright © 2025 by Micaela Elise.

MILTON & HUGO L.L.C.
4407 Park Ave., Suite 5
Union City, NJ 07087, USA

Website: *www. miltonandhugo.com*
Hotline: *1- 888-778-0033*
Email: *info@miltonandhugo.com*

Ordering Information:
Quantity sales. Special discounts are granted to corporations, associations, and other organizations. For more information on these discounts, please reach out to the publisher using the contact information provided above.

Library of Congress Control Number: 2024922346
ISBN-13:   979-8-89285-359-0   [Paperback Edition]
                  979-8-89285-360-6   [Digital Edition]

Rev. date: 01/03/2025

"It's like now that I've discovered writing I'm unstoppable. It had never occurred to me that this release could be so productive. I have always loved to write, to express myself with pretty words and imagery and anecdotes.

I guess I had taken this gift for granted. I equated it with being a good student and once I was no longer a student writing became a private, intimate activity for me alone in the dark scribbling in dozens of journals that I would never let another soul read. But here I am now seeking to publish the words I was most resistant to say.

I have the embodiment of the focal point for my shadow in this timeline to thank for that. I heard my shadow self say out loud "I'm a writer" and that triggered something in me - because I AM the writer. And I have so much to say."

1.

I still feel like a scared, insecure, lonely girl. A lot of the time.
I am fierce and passionate and capable.
Sometimes these two conflicting personas don't
make sense inside of me. As if there is not
enough space for the grand spectrum of duality.
I'm busting at the seams - my spine, my skin, my
joints all oozing, throbbing, weakening under
pressure so that there are cracks and breaks and
fissures. Releasing just enough pressure to
stall the explosion.
It is the explosion that I crave.
To burst apart in a beautiful blaze of chaos and
confetti and analyze what lays on the ground
after it all settles.
What figures will take shape? How will the landscape
fold and bend? Where will things flow?
But for now I am bottled up.
Waiting to crack.
Hoping to burst.
Filled with rage and fury and angst and confusion...
except I am too tired now to feel those things fervently.
It is exhausting being trapped in this
mechanism of a meatsuit.
To be a servant to the flesh.
Maybe the Catholics got that right and it is
people who have perverted the very words.
Maybe I'm not to give in to the flesh.
Care for it, like a garden; yes. But not give in to every whim.
I am in control after all - of this flesh at least.

Or maybe I'm not.
Knowing holding everything in will spoil my vessel -
causing disease and disdain. I have to find
release.
I have to forgive. To let go.
To let the puss of anger and resentment
flow out of the cracks.
I don't need to hold on to the poison
for grudges or for resentment.
I can move on and look forward.
I am allowed to take my time healing from things.
I don't need to move on quickly.
I do need to make the effort.
Be careful, be thoughtful, be intentional.

2.

I see the light and it feels familiar. Warm. Like it's
been waiting for me to notice. Yellow. Like it is
happy to be noticed. Bright. Like it wants to
play, to dance, just to be company.
I've had my back to the light for some time while
listening to the dark, just thumbing things over.
The dark and I have adult business to tend to. Things
that need finding and sorting. But the light
just wants time - to lounge, eat and read. The light
wants to spend time doing all my favorite
things. Frivolous things. But the dark needs my
attention... or does it? At least not all the time.
Indeed, I should spend my days outside and the
nights in contemplation. I wouldn't want to hurt
the light's feelings; I would regret it if
the light turned away from me.

3.

If I ever said "I love you" I meant it. Even if it was
only for a few minutes. Even if it was one night
out and we never saw each other again.
I loved you for that time.
And I still do.

4.

It's me. I am my problem. Not what people did to
me but the things I allowed. The situations I
put myself in. The people I gave time and energy
to who never deserved it. Maybe they deserve
kindness but it never had to come at my hand, not
at the expense of my peace. And now I walk
with their pain that was not mine but
is now transferred onto me.
I don't want it. I put it down. I forgive myself.

5.

Trust the timing. It all works out in the end. I know,
because I've been there. I came from there.
You were there too. And we are happy.

6.

you finally see my worth. after all this time and all
these trials you've deemed me worthy to love.
we've been through so much. so much that i don't
want your love anymore. the thought of being
loved by you feels like betraying myself. why would
i want you to love me, when i love myself so
much better? i love the things i love, im committed
to my goals, i want to see myself win. i
support myself more than you ever could. i love
myself in a way i don't think you've yet
experienced. in truth, i don't think you know my
value still. you've got no concept of the depth,
fervor, and power of my love - the love i've cultivated
for me. i don't even think i could show it to
you. it's just something you had to be there for, ya
know? but you weren't there. not for me. i do
hope you can show up for yourself.

7.

Chasing clarity like fireflies
Bright sparkles of light
Through the bleakness of the night
Sporadic and fleeting
Every flicker sparks bliss
Steady your focus to catch one, don't miss
As a child there were plenty
When the world was magic, and wonder
And friends were many
But the older I get
The less there are
I admit I haven't been out to look
The fields are so far
The more I know the less I understand
And clarity, like fireflies,
Escapes my searching my hands

8.

Sometimes I don't even know what it is I need to
say, I just have this longing aching desire to
speak. To talk to, relate or vent to a specific person -
but I don't know that person. It's a being.
Maybe it's me... Or my higher self. Perhaps I just
need to sit with myself a moment and discuss
how things have been on her end. What is she
going through? What are her fears? Why does
she hold on to this anger and for whom? Sometimes
I get so distracted with the busyness and
coming and goings of living in a capitalist society
that demands productivity at all hours in all
ways that I forget that she is still there.. Patiently
waiting to feel connected. To be noticed. To be
heard. But when I pause to listen she just tells me to be still.
For how long? I am restless. Will this stillness
produce something of benefit? If the stillness
provides greater productivity then sure. But to
be still for stillness sake... I fear I may have
forgotten how.
I realize this is what I long for. A moment of stillness.
Of peace. Without worry of the next task or
impending doom or "am I doing enough?" "Is
this rest justified?" It's been so long since I
enjoyed the moment in its full capacity.
Simply being. Simply present.
That is not completely true - there have been times,
but decreasingly less on my own in my own

space when I am alone with just me. I think maybe
there is a version of me that wants to be
seen in the face of death. An old version is dying. I
should spend time with her to identify exactly
what parts are dying.. What parts did they serve
and why are they no longer of service? Which
parts will fade away so that a new me may take her place?
It is time to decide. And for that, I require stillness.

9.

Why doesn't anyone talk about the anxiety that comes with stepping into your power? The overwhelming sense of it coursing through your channels, quickening your heart rate, and without the knowledge to expel or direct this power how it feels overwhelming.. Almost frightening. Nobody talks about that. They say breathe - but they don't tell you why.
In case nobody told you - that feeling is your power. Deep breathing helps.

10.

Am I tired? Is it depression? Are they different?
**Is there something fundamentally wrong with my
brain chemistry or is it perfectly normal to be**
exhausted in a world on fire, where children are
dying, women aren't safe, intelligence is
mocked, and ignorance thrives?
Am I exhausted from fighting back or from drowning?
Am I fighting? Or am I pretending? Just gliding through.
Maybe I'm not depressed or tired. Maybe I'm
unfocused. How many naps will it take to feel like I
am in control of my faculties again? Was I ever? In control, I
mean... of anything, even once? Or did I just enjoy the ride?
Sometimes I can surf on all the waves, other times
I float just on the surface, but sometimes still
**I feel like I am being dragged to the bottom. I don't
mind the bottom - at times it can be ethereal.
beautiful. captivating. But the dark gets lonely
and the pressure at these depths is crushing.**
I don't want to fight my way back up to the top, I
**don't want to abandon the darkness that wraps
me in comfort like a weighted blanket. I don't want
to come up for air. I just want to be able to
breathe while I am down here.**

11.

Turns out, I never hated the other woman.
I only hated myself for contorting my spirit to fit
into a measly underdeveloped mold with an
outdated 1950's design and no room for growth.
Turns out I don't hate you either.
I hate the bigoted societal standards that only
create shame and disdain, discouraging us all
from claiming true happiness, instead clinging
to these desperate facades to be accepted.
I've considered hating myself, for allowing so many
boundaries to be crossed and inviting in so
much heartache, or for the cruel lies I told
myself about being unlovable.
What I've realized is that a lack of love
does not equate to hate.
You don't love me, and that's ok. You don't even love yourself.
I love me. And for that, I don't need to hate anyone else.

12.

"too smart for your own good"

you cognitively understand the problems, processes,
and situations at hand so you assume that
understanding is efficient and equates to living
consciously or actively enforcing those lessons
but you neglect to actually do the work.

13.

The road to healing isn't linear. It's winding, it doubles
back on itself with loops twists and turns.
It is paved with cobblestones of grief, shame, and
even regret. The street lights flicker moments
of clarity but overwhelmingly the road is dimly lit at
best and often total darkness that forces you
to your knees feeling through the mud to stay the path.
Healing is not a chariot. There is nobody coming to
whisk you away towards the light at the end.
You have to drag yourself there bloodied and
bruised. Stand yourself back up after every trip
and stumble.
The bandaids your friends packed for you are useless
to mend the bleeding from the gashes of
your scraped knees. Every step hurts. And the whole
while you're looking back to travel forward
and that in itself is disorienting.
No, healing is not linear. It's not gentle or easy
or comforting. It is work. Necessary, white
knuckled gruesome work that straddles the paradox
of releasing, letting go and gripping tight for
dear life to your sense of self.
Healing is a sword. Double edged, singing through
the air to cut ties and release bondages and
pierces you straight to your core. Healing
hurts. That's what they don't tell you.
There is very little about the process that
is actually enjoyable. It sucks.

The other thing they don't tell you is it's not a requirement. Most people walk around their whole lives holding on to their pain. Letting it fester and manifest in an incalculable number of ways. Their unhealed parts show up in their children and grow from there taking on new life. Most people live and die without mastering a single rebirth cycle in this life and come back to do it all again in the next. Unless and until we heal that pain comes with us in every life and the lives we create.

So no, healing isn't linear or fun or comfortable or pretty. Healing is the only thing. It is the point of being human. We are all one consciousness working to heal itself.

Pls heal. I'm tired.

14.

i've always loved things with thorns.
the things that were hard to hold.
but my sister and i were only a year
apart and her thing was roses
so i had to find another thing
with thorns, or fangs, or needles
my sister loved a pretty thing
so i had to pick an ugly thing
i loved the things that bite back
i loved the unloved things
i dug love out of the mud
i let love sting me and sucked out the poison
i learned that love hurts, and that was ok
because it was MY kind of love
i loved what was left for me
i found love in the dark
i knew to love meant to be hurt
that thorns and fangs and needles
are for protection
that the things i loved in the dark
ended up there because they were denied roses
and that was ok
because we loved each other.

15.

"i'm ok"
i repeat out loud
through clenched teeth
vision blurred through hot tears
"i'm ok i'm ok"
i repeat to myself
in an attempt to calm my chest
before it collapses on itself
"i'm ok i'm ok i'm ok"
i repeat in vain
as i hyperventilate
struggling to find the rhythm of a steady breath
"i'm ok i'm ok i'm ok i'm ok"
i repeat to my inner child
rocking us both gently on the floor
until one of us falls asleep.

16.

My blood is made up of almost two dozen beautifully
rich cultures that were colonized and
plundered and tainted with the blood of their
oppressors. I was born from the rage of women,
whose screams echo in the chambers
of my heart, and the sin of man.
My breath bubbled up from the soils
stained with tears wept for lost sons.
I walk with the copper, iron and ore of the
Earth from every continent in my bones.
The salt of the sea alchemizes in my muscles and
tendons, driving me forward with purpose,
each step lit by the heat of the sun absorbed in my
skin as the catalyst that pushes me forward;
and its message is carried in the winds.
I am here for liberation and retribution.

17.

If you kill bugs
Do not preach to me about the righteousness of your faith
I have no interest in your misguided theology

18.

"Strong" no longer feels like a compliment. I
stopped listing it as a positive attribute.
I resent how strong I had to become. I would
prefer to not have to show my strength.

My strength has teeth. It keeps rage on a short
leash, penned up with a loose lock. My strength
is vengeful. She's developed a blood lust from battle.

Strength comes with a crushing weight. The muscle,
the armor, the sword - it's all heavy. I'd like
to set down strength for a while and cultivate peace instead.

The problem is, my strength is very protective of
my peace. She will raise her axe at the first
sign of disturbance. Tread carefully with me. Please
be gentle with my peace. I need a break
from being strong.

19.

"I invite ___ into my heart and soul."
"I am a humble servant to do ___'s work."
"Serve ___ with all your heart and all your soul."
"Then they said to __, "What shall we do, that we
may work the works of __?" ___ answered
and said to them, "This is the work of __, that you
believe in __ whom He sent." for it is __ who
works in you both to will and to do for His good pleasure."

**Servitude in exchange for the promise of everlasting
life … a contract in which your soul is the**
currency and fulfillment of the promise is unfounded.

When I die, return my body to the soil. Return my
breath to the wind. Return my blood to the
**rain and give my tears to the sea.
My soul I will keep. I will not be sold to any deity.
The rivers and the trees have never asked this of me.**

20.

I spent every summer outside
Climbing trees and wading in streams
Through every season of my life
Every heartbreak, disappointment, failure
I would find my way back to the trees
Sit under a big tall oak just to breathe
After loss and uncertainty
Through addiction and disease
When overcoming abuse
The one constant, stable thing
has always been the trees
Never judging. Always listening
Delivering comfort as light whispers on the breeze

21.

i start to feel good and i want to share that with you
i want to show you how much better i am
i want you to see my smile feel my joy
rest in this peace with me together

so i call you over
you come

but now i'm anxious

if you had only been here 15 minutes
ago... when you weren't here ..
then you would see me put together

instead you are here and i am a mess.
my anxiety walked in the door with you.

i didn't get a chance to tell you all my good news,
i was too busy straightening out the things i missed
(thankfully you were here to point them out)

ok, so it's not as perfect as it seemed when
i explained to you on the phone...

but look! here - i've done something else well
ok, not "well." i guess you're right, it could be better ...

but i'm working on it. aren't you proud?

i have to admit, i see your point.
it's not as great as i made it sound.

things did seem a lot better
when you were not around

22.

i'm looking forward to some regulation
something to tip the scale toward normal
just a little something to take the edge off
to calm and quiet the monkey on my back
that howls and dances with knives in his hands
stabbing me in the head and neck
again and again
just a little sedative
not enough to make him sleep
just make him content
to stop stomping his feet
you think you can do that ?
find a pill that fits right
for my particularly special plight?
I'm not like the others
I already know my demons
I just need a little help
swimming back from the deep end

23.

Stop punishing yourself
The way the light shines through the leaves is beautiful
Take a look
That's for you and you didn't have to
do a single thing to deserve it
You can enjoy life simply because you are alive
Unclench your jaw. Let your shoulders fall.
The sun came out today and it is just
as powerful as its ever been
It shines to keep you alive and dapple
your body in soft warm kisses
You are here now and that's all the sun requires of you
It will rise again tomorrow and love you
the same as it has for millenia
You didn't do anything to earn that. You'll never have to.
Don't be nervous. You are allowed to receive.
Lift your head
You are worthy, brilliant, exalted and
should be showered in blessings
Even before you take any action you
are surrounded by abundance
It exists all around you whether you acknowledge it or not.
Your presence is welcomed here, now.
Everything in existence has conspired for you to be here
All you have to do is be.

24.

The wind does not struggle through air
Nor should you struggle through life
Take as many breaths as you'd like

25.

Something about you thinking I'm pussy just sets me off.
No, I can't let it go. How dare you suggest I'm soft.
I don't care that now it's a "joke" and it's
not that I have something to prove
But I've been a born fighter, it's what they created me to do.
I don't need any weapons, slick words,
or a battery in my back
I can conjure rage like no other these are spiritual attacks
My fury is divine like nothing you've seen
And losing my shit is one of my favorite things
I'm a gladiator that's been trained from very young age
Hands up. Chin tucked. Keep a wide stance
Kill or be killed is just the name of the dance

26.

It's okay
That I never found my footing in my mother's hometown
Because I became a child of the world instead
I am a myriad of all the cultures, people,
and places that took me in
A collection of phrases in different languages,
of art pieces in mixed forms of media
It's true, my seat at the family table was vacated long ago
But I found warmth at the hearth of community
Many communities, in fact.
A house mother in juvie taught me to
make tostones & empanadas
My children love them, and we share her love by extension
I sing in spanish and eat homemade ramen with chopsticks
prefer my curry with chickpeas over chicken
I know where to harvest red willow, and when to use it
So many gifts have been shared to make me who I am
So many hands have lent wisdom to get me where I am
How could I ever be so ungrateful to
wish for anything different
My roots found the richest, deepest of soils
In the most beautiful people from every corner of the world

27.

I need to pull the thoughts out of me
Like a string of pearls
One by one lightening the load
This treasured chest filled with not only a
heart and lungs but words, and wisdom
Pull harder and it pops like a plug
Draining the swamp...
It reminds me of a lake in Florida
I forget the name but in the native language it
means "disappearing waters". The lake is situated
above limestone sinkholes and every few decades
the whole thing empties. If you weren't
expecting it, it would be terrifying. It would seem
like an ecological disaster, the water levels
dropping inches by the hour.
But if you have spent generations there than you know
It is not a disaster, it is a rebirth. A death cycle
necessary for the ecosystem to thrive.
Whole deer being swallowed up by the swirling
waters and other large debris eventually block
up the sinkholes and the ground
resembles something solid again.
As their bodies decompose they provide an abundance
of rich nutrients that nurture the grasses
and other vegetation of what is now a marsh
instead of a lake. Scavengers feast. Insects
prevail. As the years go by the offspring of the
wildlife know this land to be of milk and honey -

lush, green, plentiful. The birds come for the bugs,
the deer come for the grass. Eventually the
water returns and with it the predators. In another
decade the offspring of the wildlife and the
people in the area will know this land to be a pond.
Then a lake. And it will remain that way -
with boaters, fisherman, and swimming; transformed
into an utterly different ecosystem. Until
the ground gives way, and the death/
rebirth cycle begins again.
I think about this lake a lot.
I search for the sinkholes in my mind. Soft spots
where maybe things will begin flowing through.
Where will the thoughts pour from so
that I may die and be reborn?
The lake of my mind is more of a swamp and
the water is murky. It smells of sulfur and
stagnation.
Then, without warning, the bottom gives out. A
dam breaks. There is movement and that is
where I send all my attention - accidentally and
inadvertently sealing the break with the sheer
amount of energy I've sent to the site.
The trick is to let it flow, I think. To surrender.
Let it fall apart. Then let it all work out.

28.

You understand things from your perspective
That doesn't invalidate my experience
I'm not sorry that my push back on your
narrative makes you uncomfortable
In fact, I hope it makes your skin crawl and
the hair on your neck stand up
Twists your gut so that it churns mud and bricks
Sours your tongue leaving a rotten taste and
thick sludge that gets caught in your throat
Forcing your eyes to well up with cloudy tears from
the overwhelming nauseating sensation to
vomit
And as you double over, clawing at your neck and
grasping at the vulnerable flesh of your belly,
you choke on it.

29.

Duality exists in all things
It is ever pervasive
Existence itself cannot exist without the concept of nothing
The goal is not to deny any part of you
But to integrate every part of you.
To be healed is to be balanced.

30.

I can't wait to meet with God and compare notes.
Sis, what were you thinking? You're wild for that.

Burn After Writing

These pages are included for you to discover the cathartic release of putting pen to paper. If you are not ready to share your vulnerabilities, dreams, secrets, or desires with the world you can always tear out the page and burn after writing

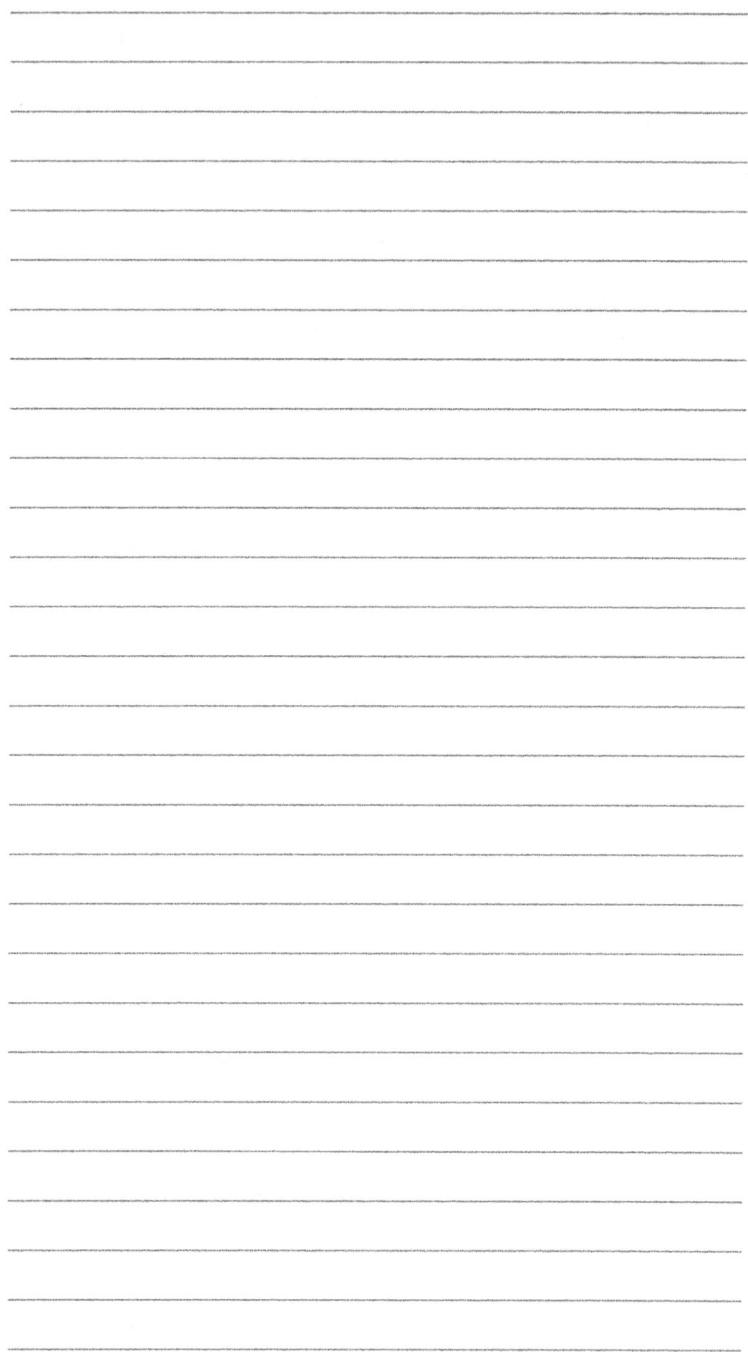